A FLAG FOR JUNETEENTH

Kim Taylor

NEAL PORTER BOOKS

HOLIDAY HOUSE / NEW YORK

To my beautiful daughter Mikayla,
whose smile can outshine the brightest sunbeam.

Neal Porter Books

Text and illustrations copyright © 2023 by Kim Taylor

All Rights Reserved

HOLIDAY HOUSE is registered in the U.S. Patent and Trademark Office.

Printed and bound in April 2023 at C&C Offset, Shenzhen, China.

The artwork for this book was created with

fabric collage using raw edge applique and free motion quilting.

Book design by Jennifer Browne

www.holidayhouse.com

First Edition

3 5 7 9 10 8 6 4 2

Library of Congress Cataloging-in-Publication Data is available.

ISBN: 978-0-8234-5224-8 (hardcover)

The scent of nutmeg and vanilla floated through our cabin...

...and landed as a smile on my face. Tea cakes smell so good while they are baking that I can taste them before I even take the first bite!

Tomorrow is June 19, 1865, my tenth birthday.
Mama said that I am practically a grown-up.
"Huldah, go to bed now. You have a big
day tomorrow."

I thought I was dreaming when I heard the loud clip-clippity-clop of heavy horses' hooves. Mama and Papa sat up, rubbing their tired eyes. Worried faces peeked out from cabin windows and doors.

Dusty soldiers crowded into the little corner of the Texas
plantation where we lived. A man with a beard jumped down
from his horse and held a paper up high for all to see.
With a booming voice, he read,

"The people of Texas are informed that, in accordance with a proclamation from the President of the United States, all slaves are free."

I held my breath. No one said a word. Then
cheers, louder than the loudest thunder!

The angry plantation owners followed the soldiers as they rode away, shouting questions at their backs. We didn't know it, but President Abraham Lincoln had signed the Emancipation Proclamation more than two years earlier. Enslaved people had been free since then, but the plantation owners chose not to tell us.

I squeezed through the crowd, listening as people prayed, sang, and cried quiet tears of joy.

The noise woke baby Eve, who made her own loud fuss. I opened my cabin door with a hand that looked new to me. I hugged my sweet baby sister while songs of freedom filled the air outside.

Baby Eve blinked in the bright sunshine. A group of excited women made plans as they sewed freedom flags. Eve and I watched as their hands made quick, perfect stitches. Many looked like the patchwork quilts that kept us warm at night. Jacob Menard, the oldest man on the plantation, hobbled to the center of the square. He held his walking stick high in the air.

"Today is a jubilee! A day to celebrate our freedom!"

Laughing children searched for smooth tree branches
to use as flagpoles.

"Find a stick! Find a stick! Not too thin, not too thick!"

"Make a flag for all to see! Make a flag for Jubilee!"

Papa and the other men carved the branches with beautiful designs.

"Papa, what does that mean?" I asked, pointing.

His finger made an outline of the carved-out space.

"This symbol is called *Fawohodie*. It means independence and freedom."

It was just then that I remembered my birthday!
"Papa, I'll be back soon."
I took the long way into the woods . . .

around the pond,

over the pile of smooth stones,

and through the tall grass.

I found my favorite tree
and climbed until I could
see the horizon.

I felt hopeful and very grown-up.
I pulled a small jar with a lid from
my pocket. Bright sunbeams were
shining through the leaves. I
grabbed one and carefully put
it in my little jar.

When I made it back to the plantation, Mama was waiting for me.

"Huldah, where have you been? It's time to start your birthday celebration!"

I showed her the little jar of light and explained that I had captured a sunbeam.

"Huldah, put on your beautiful birthday dress and meet me outside. I have a surprise for you."

Everyone sat around me in a big circle and Mr. Menard handed me a large sack tied with a pretty ribbon. I opened it. My own freedom flag!

Mr. Menard said, "Everyone on the plantation helped sew it. But it isn't finished yet."

My flag was a patchwork of soft yellow and green with a purple stripe across the middle.

"Huldah," Mama said, "this white star represents our right to freedom. Please sew it into your flag." She handed me a needle and my little jar.

I placed the star so that
it rose from the purple stripe like a
sunrise. I sewed in the bright sunbeam so that
it could help to guide me wherever I might take it.

That night, as our neighbors returned to their cabins, Mama and Papa whispered to me that they had planned something special just for us. We held hands as we walked into the woods.

Mama and Papa hugged me. "Happy birthday, Huldah! Happy Jubilee Day."

We looked up at the moonlit sky as the tall trees smiled down at us. Mama and Papa wrapped baby Eve in my beautiful flag. They held her high, and together, we owned our freedom.

A NOTE FROM THE AUTHOR

When Barack Obama was elected 44th president of the United States in 2008, I was hit with a rush of emotions that I found difficult to process. I felt excited, proud, and awed that an African American man had won the presidency in this country. I wanted to express my feelings artistically, in a way that would help me to feel connected to my ancestors while marking this historic moment. I found myself thinking about how women in Central and West Africa were master weavers and textile artists. During their enslavement, African American women created beautiful quilts with embedded codes to lead others to freedom along the Underground Railroad. They made quilts out of scraps to keep their families warm, and created beautiful story quilts that recorded ancestral history and family memories. I knew this was how I wanted to tell my own stories. I taught myself to quilt. My first story quilt, *Full Circle, A History*, was created in honor of Barack Obama's incredible achievement in a country where slavery was once a legal institution.

In 2014, I attended a local Juneteenth celebration. There was delicious soul food, folk music, and poetry readings. Vendors were selling jewelry, and people talked excitedly about recent trips to Africa. Until that day, I had never heard of Juneteenth. I was not taught about it in school, and the elders in my family did not celebrate it. As soon as I got home I devoured everything I could read about Juneteenth. I was so moved that I decided to create a story quilt. I was thrilled that it was exhibited at various local venues and at a few schools. Most of the students that I spoke to did not know the story of Juneteenth. I was saddened that it was not part of school curriculum. I wrote a short story as an accompaniment to my quilt to help students connect to this important event in history.

When the pandemic hit in 2020, I decided to revise my Juneteenth story. I felt that the timing was perfect. Like people all over the country and the world, I was stuck at home. There was buzz that Juneteenth would soon be recognized as a federal holiday, and I was itching to do something creative! I also felt the weight of telling this story to children. I wanted my story to emphasize the strength, wisdom, and resilience of enslaved people. I wanted to demonstrate the importance of community, family love, and the recognition of ancestral ties even in the face of the atrocities of that time. I wanted to show that slavery was imposed upon, but did not define, Africans or African Americans. I wanted young readers to come away with a feeling of pride, and to see art as a means of cultural preservation. There is also much symbolism to be found throughout the story, from the names of the characters, to the African concept that it takes a village to raise a child.

It is my artistic signature that my quilted characters have no faces. When I was young, I was an avid reader. I loved using my imagination to decide what the characters looked like. When creating the illustrations for this book, I was excited to explore ways to demonstrate feelings such as love, emotional connection, and joy without depicting facial expression. I wanted readers to see themselves in the characters and to connect with them on a deeper level. *A Flag for Juneteenth* also introduces young readers to the art of flag designing (vexillography). I hope they will be inspired to make their own freedom flags!

The quilted illustrations for this book took a little over a year to complete. I am deeply grateful to my agents, Regina Brooks and Charles Kim at Serendipity Literary Agency, for encouraging me to illustrate the story using quilts, and to editor Neal Porter and art director Jennifer Browne for allowing me to fully express myself in this book. And to my readers, I can only hope that the love I put into creating *A Flag for Juneteenth* resonates with you.

Kim Taylor